BRYCE HARPER

SPORTS SUPERSTARS

BY THOMAS K. ADAMSON

BELLWETHER MEDIA • MINNEAPOLIS, MN

Torque brims with excitement perfect for thrill-seekers of all kinds. Discover daring survival skills, explore uncharted worlds, and marvel at mighty engines and extreme sports. In *Torque* books, anything can happen. Are you ready?

This edition first published in 2024 by Bellwether Media, Inc.

No part of this publication may be reproduced in whole or in part without written permission of the publisher. For information regarding permission, write to Bellwether Media, Inc., Attention: Permissions Department, 6012 Blue Circle Drive, Minnetonka, MN 55343.

Library of Congress Cataloging-in-Publication Data

Names: Adamson, Thomas K., 1970- author.
Title: Bryce Harper / by Thomas K. Adamson.
Description: Minneapolis, MN : Bellwether Media, Inc., 2024. | Series: Torque: Sports superstars | Includes bibliographical references and index. | Audience: Ages 7-12 years | Audience: Grades 2-3 | Summary: "Engaging images accompany information about the life and accomplishments of Bryce Harper. The combination of high- interest subject matter and light text is intended for students in grades 3 through 7"- Provided by publisher.
Identifiers: LCCN 2023040012 (print) | LCCN 2023040013 (ebook) | ISBN 9798886878288 (library binding) | ISBN 9798886879223 (ebook)
Subjects: LCSH: Harper, Bryce, 1992–Juvenile literature. | Outfielders (Baseball)–United States–Biography–Juvenile literature. | Baseball players–United States–Biography–Juvenile literature. | Washington Nationals (Baseball team)–History–Juvenile literature. | Philadelphia Phillies (Baseball team)–History–Juvenile literature. | Major League Baseball (Organization)–Juvenile literature.
Classification: LCC GV865.H268 A43 2024 (print) | LCC GV865.H268 (ebook) | DDC 796.357092 [B]–dc23/eng/20231012
LC record available at https://lccn.loc.gov/2023040012

Text copyright © 2024 by Bellwether Media, Inc. TORQUE and associated logos are trademarks and/or registered trademarks of Bellwether Media, Inc.

Editor: Rebecca Sabelko   Designer: Gabriel Hilger

Printed in the United States of America, North Mankato, MN.

TABLE OF CONTENTS

HARPER'S BIG HOME RUN	4
WHO IS BRYCE HARPER?	6
A TALENTED TEENAGER	8
BECOMING A SUPERSTAR	12
HARPER'S GOALS	20
GLOSSARY	22
TO LEARN MORE	23
INDEX	24

HARPER'S BIG HOME RUN

It is Game 5 of the 2022 **championship** series for the **National League** (NL). The Philadelphia Phillies are down by one late in the game.

Bryce Harper is batting with a runner on base. The pitch speeds toward Harper. He swings and hits a **home run**! The Phillies go on to win the game. They are on their way to the **World Series**!

2022 NATIONAL LEAGUE CHAMPION

WHO IS BRYCE HARPER?

Bryce Harper is an **outfielder** in **Major League Baseball** (MLB). He plays for the Philadelphia Phillies.

Getting National Attention

Harper was on a 2009 cover of *Sports Illustrated* magazine. He was only 16 years old!

BRYCE HARPER

BIRTHDAY October 16, 1992

HOMETOWN Las Vegas, Nevada

POSITION outfielder and designated hitter

HEIGHT 6 feet 3 inches

DRAFTED Washington Nationals in the 1st round (1st overall) of the 2010 MLB Draft

Harper is a skilled hitter with a powerful swing. His Phillies teammates call him "The Showman." He got this nickname because he makes key hits when the team needs them.

A TALENTED TEENAGER

Harper began playing baseball when he was 3 years old. He played against older kids. At age 9, he began playing on travel teams. He played against many talented, older kids throughout the United States.

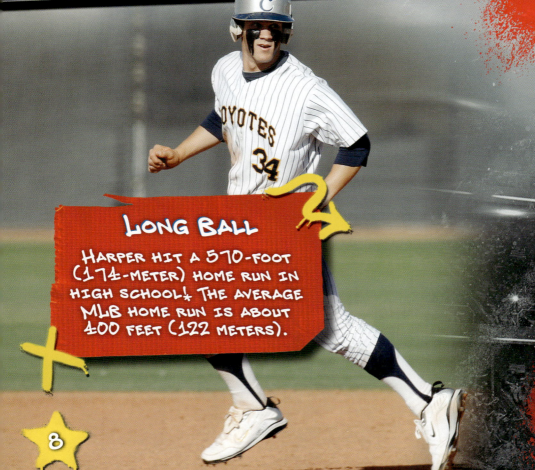

Long Ball

Harper hit a 570-foot (174-meter) home run in high school! The average MLB home run is about 400 feet (122 meters).

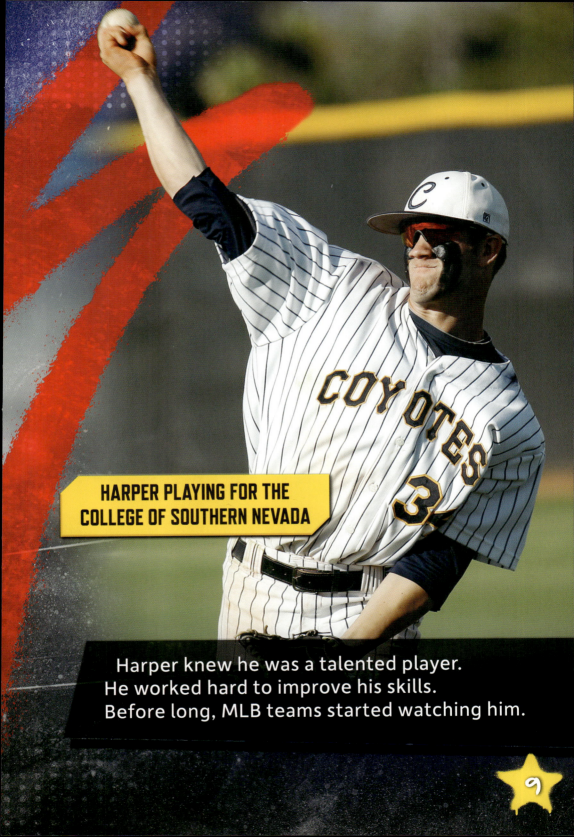

HARPER PLAYING FOR THE COLLEGE OF SOUTHERN NEVADA

Harper knew he was a talented player. He worked hard to improve his skills. Before long, MLB teams started watching him.

Harper finished high school early. He began playing baseball at the College of Southern Nevada. He hoped to play against more skilled players. But he outplayed everyone.

The Washington Nationals picked Harper first in the 2010 **draft**. In 2011, he played in their **minor league** system. He faced better pitching. But he still batted well.

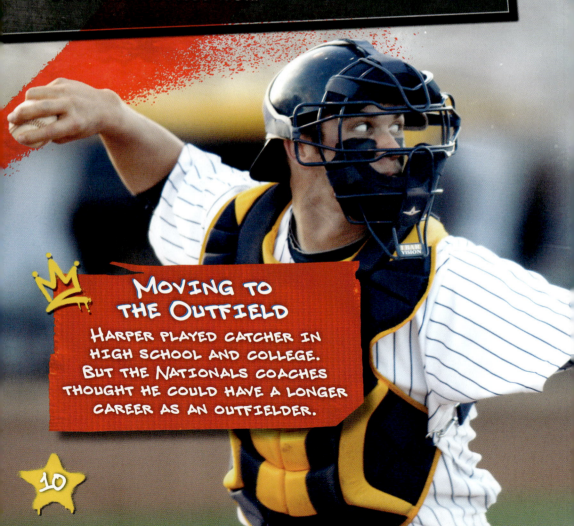

Moving to the Outfield

Harper played catcher in high school and college. But the Nationals coaches thought he could have a longer career as an outfielder.

FAVORITES

FOOD: steak

FOOTBALL TEAM: Philadelphia Eagles

MUSICIAN: Elvis Presley

CEREAL: Cheerios

11

BECOMING A SUPERSTAR

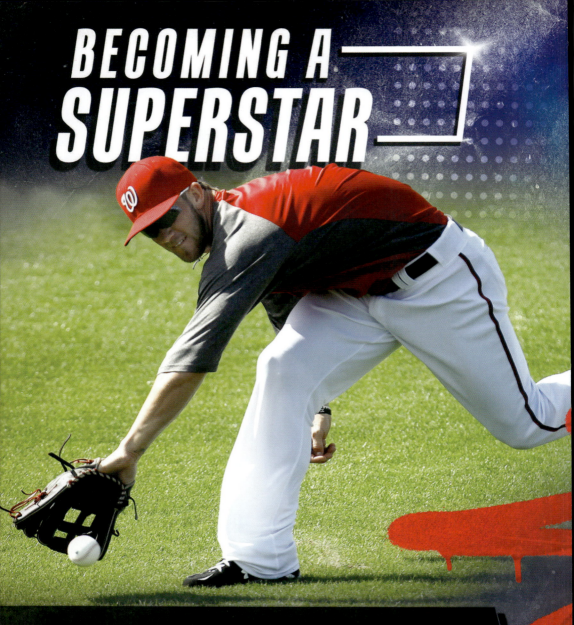

Harper was only 19 years old at the start of the 2012 season. He began playing on the Nationals top minor league team. But he did not stay there long. They called him up in April.

Harper had a great **rookie** season with the Nationals. He hit 22 home runs. He won NL Rookie of the Year.

Harper struggled with injuries in 2013 and 2014. He missed many games. But he played well when he was healthy.

Harper came back strong in 2015. He tied for the most home runs in the NL with 42. He became the youngest player to win every vote for the NL's **Most Valuable Player** (MVP) award. He continued his strong play from 2016 to 2018.

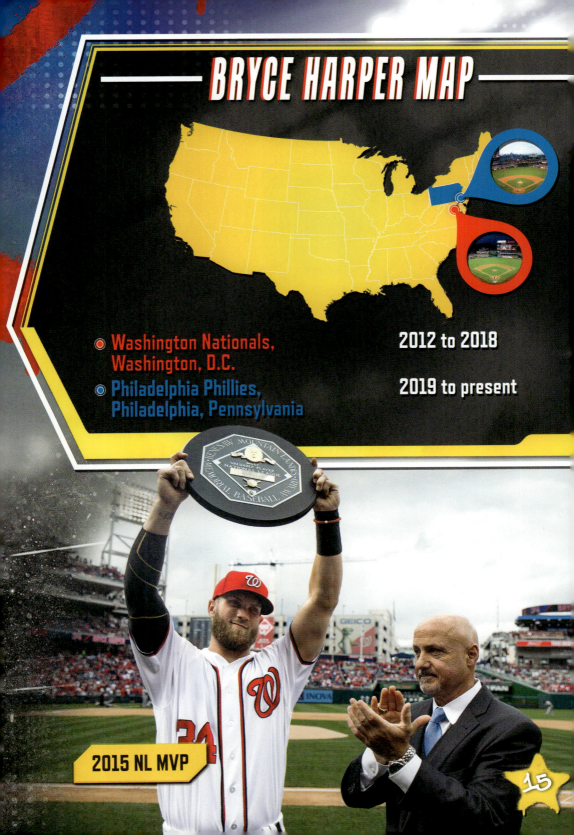

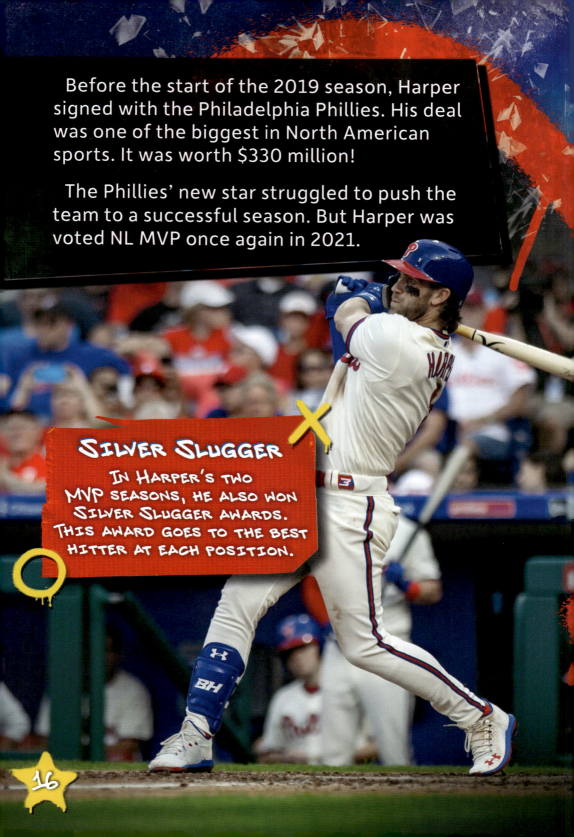

Before the start of the 2019 season, Harper signed with the Philadelphia Phillies. His deal was one of the biggest in North American sports. It was worth $330 million!

The Phillies' new star struggled to push the team to a successful season. But Harper was voted NL MVP once again in 2021.

Silver Slugger

In Harper's two MVP seasons, he also won Silver Slugger awards. This award goes to the best hitter at each position.

Harper started strong in 2022. But he missed many games because of injuries. Harper hurt his elbow in May. He could not throw. He became a **designated hitter**.

In June, a pitch hit his thumb. He had to have surgery. But he recovered in time to help the Phillies reach the World Series. Unfortunately, they lost the series.

TIMELINE

— 2010 —
Harper is drafted by the Nationals

— April 2012 —
Harper plays in his first MLB game

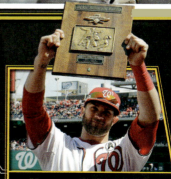

— November 2012 —
Harper wins NL Rookie of the Year

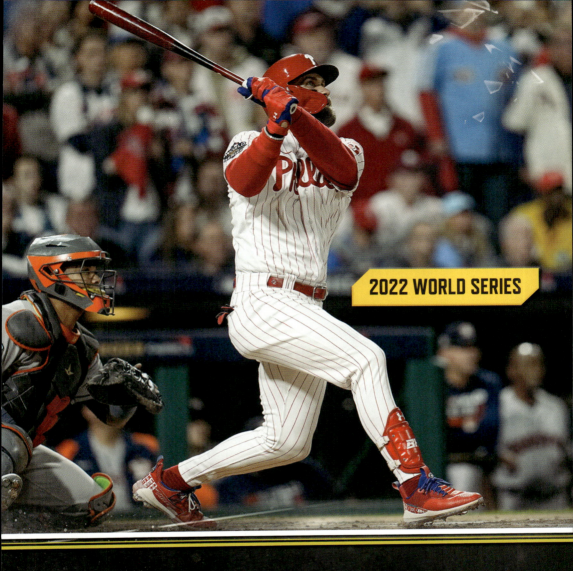

2022 WORLD SERIES

— 2015 —
Harper wins his first NL MVP award

— 2019 —
Harper signs with the Phillies

— 2021 —
Harper wins his second NL MVP award

19

HARPER'S GOALS

Harper started a program called Harper's Heroes. It raises money for children's blood cancer research. Kids get to go to a game and meet Harper.

Harper has big goals for his future. He believes he can play baseball until he is 45 years old. He wants to be one of the best players ever!

GLOSSARY

championship—a contest to decide the best team or person

designated hitter—a player on a baseball team that only hits and does not play in the field

draft—a process where professional teams choose high school and college athletes to play for them

home run—a hit where the batter runs all the way around the bases and scores a run; home runs are usually hit over the outfield fence.

Major League Baseball—a professional baseball league in the United States; Major League Baseball is often called MLB.

minor league—a professional baseball league below Major League Baseball

most valuable player—the best player in a year, game, or series; the most valuable player is often called the MVP.

National League—one of the two large groupings of teams in Major League Baseball; the other is the American League.

outfielder—a position in baseball where a player stands far away from the batter to catch baseballs that are hit high into the air

rookie—a first-year player in a sports league

World Series—the championship series in Major League Baseball, played between the best team in the American League and the best team in the National League

TO LEARN MORE

AT THE LIBRARY

Aretha, David. *Trout vs. Harper vs. Betts vs. Ruth.* New York, N.Y.: Rosen Publishing, 2020.

Hewson, Anthony K. *Philadelphia Phillies.* Minneapolis, Minn.: Abdo Publishing, 2023.

Pike, Jeremy. *Bryce Harper.* Hollywood, Fla.: Mason Crest, 2024.

ON THE WEB

Factsurfer.com gives you a safe, fun way to find more information.

1. Go to www.factsurfer.com

2. Enter "Bryce Harper" into the search box and click 🔍.

3. Select your book cover to see a list of related content.

INDEX

awards, 4, 13, 14, 15, 16, 17
catcher, 10
childhood, 6, 8, 9, 10
College of Southern Nevada, 9, 10
deal, 16
designated hitter, 18
draft, 10
favorites, 11
future, 21
Harper's Heroes, 20
home run, 4, 8, 13, 14
injuries, 14, 18
Major League Baseball, 6, 8, 9
map, 15

minor league, 10, 12
Most Valuable Player, 14, 15, 16, 17
National League, 4, 13, 14, 15, 16, 17
nickname, 7
outfielder, 6, 10
Philadelphia Phillies, 4, 6, 7, 16, 18
profile, 7
Rookie of the Year, 13
Silver Slugger Award, 16
timeline, 18–19
trophy shelf, 17
Washington Nationals, 10, 12, 13
World Series, 4, 18, 19

The images in this book are reproduced through the courtesy of: Matt Slocum/ AP Images/ AP Newsroom, front cover, pp. 4, 4-5, 7 (Bryce Harper); Cal Sport Media/ Alamy, pp. 3, 23; Joe Robbins/ Icon Sportswire/ AP Images/ AP Newsroom, p. 6; Charlie Neibergall/ AP Images/ AP Newsroom, p. 7 (logo); Isaac Brekken/ AP Images/ AP Newsroom, pp. 8, 9, 10-11; MaraZe, p. 11 (steak); NFL/ Wiki Commons, p. 11 (Eagles logo); Shawshots, p. 11 (Elvis Presley); Moving Moment, p. 11 (Cheerios); Mike Janes/ AP Images/ AP Newsroom, p. 11 (Bryce Harper); Julio Cortez/ AP Images/ AP Newsroom, p. 12; Jeff Roberson/ AP Images/ AP Newsroom, p. 13; Four Seam Images/ AP Images/ AP Newsroom, p. 14; AgnosticPreachersKid/ Wiki Commons, p. 15 (Nationals Stadium); Frank Romeo, p. 15 (Phillies Stadium); Evan Vucci/ AP Images/ AP Newsroom, p. 15 (2015 NL MVP); John Jones/ Icon Sportswire/ AP Images/ AP Newsroom, p. 16; Laurence Kesterson/ AP Images/ AP Newsroom, p. 17; Derrick Tuskan/ AP Images/ AP Newsroom, p. 18 (injury); Alex Brandon/ AP Images/ AP Newsroom, p. 18 (NL Rookie of the Year); MLB/ Wiki Commons, pp. 18 (Nationals logo), 19 (Phillies logo); David J. Phillip/ AP Images/ AP Newsroom, p. 19 (Bryce Harper); ASSOCIATED PRESS/ AP Images/ AP Newsroom, p. 20; Rich Graessle/ Icon Sportswire/ AP Images/ AP Newsroom, p. 21.